COLUMBUS

IMPRESSIONS

photography by Randall Lee Schieber

foreword by Robin Smith

FARCOUNTRY
PRESS

Right: The Hyatt on Capitol Square (at left) sits at the corner of Third and State streets, across from the Ohio Statehouse.

Far right: The Ohio Statehouse nestles in the center of Capitol Square, a ten-acre green space surrounded by the office towers of modern-day Columbus.

Title page: Magnolias bloom on the campus of Trinity Lutheran Seminary in Bexley. Trinity and Capital University's adjacent campuses are Bexley landmarks.

Front cover: The Scioto riverfront and downtown Columbus twinkle with light in this evening view. The fountains of John W. Galbreath Bicentennial Park dance in the foreground, while Civic Center Drive meanders past the Promenade on the Scioto Mile to the Discovery Bridge. The LeVeque Tower glows red, white, and blue at center.

Back cover: Cyclists enjoy an afternoon ride along the Scioto Greenway at North Bank Park. The Greenway follows the Scioto River through downtown Columbus, winding through Alexander AEP Park, Battelle Riverfront Park, the Scioto Mile, John W. Galbreath Bicentennial Park, and Scioto Audubon Park.

ISBN 10: 1-56037-513-2
ISBN 13: 978-1-56037-513-5

© 2011 by Farcountry Press
Photography © 2011 by Randall Lee Schieber

For more information about our books, write Farcountry Press, P.O. Box 5630, Helena, MT 59604; call (800) 821-3874; or visit www.farcountrypress.com.

Created, produced, and designed in the United States.
Printed in China.

16 15 14 13 12 11   1 2 3 4 5 6

COLUMBUS

by Robin Smith

There was a time when those who visited or moved to Columbus did not expect to fall in love with the place. The long-overlooked middle sibling of the "3-C" triumvirate of Cleveland, Columbus, and Cincinnati, Columbus was the last to be founded—not until 1812—and might never have existed at all if the founders of Franklinton (a town located across the Scioto River that had long since been absorbed into the city) had not offered to donate both land and $50,000 dollars' worth of buildings to the state to establish the new state capital on the eastern river bluffs. Columbus had a lot of catching up to do.

No more. Columbus has not only outstripped its big brothers in population but it grew by more than 10 percent in the past decade, while Cleveland and Cincinnati each shrank significantly. Columbus is now by far the largest city in Ohio, and it continues to grow.

Why? Many are drawn here by the business community and the prospect of jobs. Columbus is home to no less than five major insurance companies, as well as major retail chains, banks, and health organizations. And, of course, government has a large employment presence: the combined city, county, state, and federal employers provide the largest pool of jobs in the area. Others come for the education: The Ohio State University is its own city within the city, and there are several fine private schools, technical colleges, and a thriving community college.

The Discovery Bridge carries Broad Street across the Scioto River into downtown Columbus. At left, the forty-seven-story LeVeque Tower glows softly. This art deco masterpiece has graced the Columbus skyline since 1927, and it remained the tallest building in the city until 1974.

But if jobs and education draw people, it's the vibrancy of the city that makes them stay. Simply put, Columbus *rocks*. This is a diverse, colorful, upbeat city with distinct and interesting neighborhoods and activities for everyone. You want high culture? Try the world-class Columbus Museum of Art, the Columbus Symphony Orchestra, or the BalletMet. You want funky and cutting-edge? The Short North Arts District's galleries, street fairs, and entertainment venues are your places to go. Sports are huge in Columbus, from Ohio State Buckeyes football to the National Hockey League's Columbus Blue Jackets to Minor League Baseball's Columbus Clippers— and for those who prefer their sports participatory, there are terrific facilities throughout the area.

While offering plenty of entertainment in the present, Columbus has not forgotten its past. The Ohio Historical Society is headquartered here, and Columbus boasts a significant historical preservation community, working to protect the best of the past as the city grows. Perhaps the largest and best-known preservation project of recent years was the complete renovation of Ohio's historic Statehouse, completed in 1996, but the people of Columbus have also worked to save beautiful theaters, train stations, homes, and dozens of other historically or architecturally significant buildings.

And Columbus knows how to have *fun*. The neon glitz of the Ohio State Fair, the color and ethnic accents of the Irish, Greek, Latino, and Asian festivals, the lingering counterculture vibe of ComFest, and the quirky hilarity of the Doo Dah Parade all reveal a city that knows how to kick back and have a good time. And in sharing the fun and culture of this diverse and surprising city— at its heart still a friendly Midwestern town where people say hello on the street and children play in downtown fountains—visitors and residents alike often find that Columbus has stolen their hearts.

It is indeed a privilege to introduce the Columbus impressions of photographer Randall Lee Schieber. A longtime resident of Columbus, Randall captures the best of the city: its color and excitement, its inspired silliness, its beauty, and its meditations on the past. You, too, will be impressed by this city that so many have come to love. Welcome.

Robin Smith Is a writer and graphic designer based in Columbus, Ohio. Her publications include *Columbus Ghosts, Columbus Ghosts II,* and *Ohio Then and Now* (with Randall Lee Schieber).

Left: Buckeye Nation gathers in front of Ohio Stadium on the campus of The Ohio State University. The Ohio State Buckeyes have played football in the distinctively shaped "Horseshoe" since their inaugural game against Ohio Wesleyan on October 7, 1922. Extensive renovations have made the 'Shoe the fourth-largest on-campus stadium in the country, with a seating capacity of 102,329.

Below: The Muirfield Village Golf Club in Dublin has hosted the PGA's Memorial Tournament since 1976. Designed by Columbus-native Jack Nicklaus, the course is consistently rated among the top-twenty golf venues in the United States and has welcomed golf luminaries including Greg Norman, Tiger Woods, Hale Irwin, Fred Couples, and Ernie Els.

Bottom: Major League Soccer's Columbus Crew began play on April 13, 1996, at Ohio Stadium. In 1999 they moved to their current home pitch, Crew Stadium—the first soccer-specific stadium built in the United States. Here the Crew battles the Chicago Fire.

Right: Students enjoy a crisp fall day at Mirror Lake at The Ohio State University. A landmark since the campus opened in 1873, Mirror Lake was once spring-fed and used as a source of drinking water. Campus expansion dried up the spring in the 1920s; today the lake holds 91,000 cubic feet of well, river, and city water.

Below: A ninety-four-acre island of green along the Scioto River, the Scioto Audubon Metro Park occupies reclaimed industrial land on the Whittier Peninsula south of downtown. Seven wetland cells and the river itself attract a variety of water birds including wood ducks, sandpipers, herons, and egrets. Anchored by the Grange Insurance Audubon Center, an 18,000-square-foot "green" facility built with recycled construction materials, the park features bike and jogging trails, fishing, boating, and the largest free outdoor climbing wall in the United States.

8

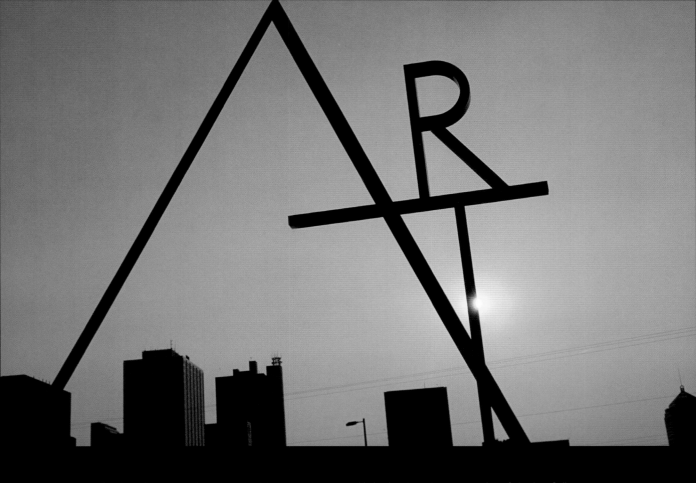

Above: Framing an evening view of downtown Columbus, the Art sign provides a graphic landmark on the campus of the Columbus College of Art and Design. From its position straddling East Gay Street, the bright-red declaration can be seen from blocks away.

Facing page: Dusk accentuates the burnished surfaces of Stephen Canneto's *NavStar* at Franklin Park Conservatory and Botanical Gardens. Inspired by the shape of the sextant, a navigational instrument used by sailors, the three triangular forms become the billowing sails of ships. The easternmost "sail" points to the North Star.

Above: The bright lights of the Short North Arts District beckon on a summer night. Located between downtown and the Ohio State campus, the Short North features an eclectic mix of galleries, shopping, dining, and entertainment, and its monthly Gallery Hop has been a Columbus tradition for more than twenty-five years. Overlooking the busy scene is the Greater Columbus Convention Center.

Right: The Ohio Theatre was built in 1928 as a Loew's movie theater. Nearly demolished in 1969, it inspired a grassroots preservation campaign that raised more than $2 million in less than a year. The Spanish Baroque gem is now managed by the Columbus Association for the Performing Arts (CAPA), and it hosts performances ranging from Broadway productions to CAPA's popular Summer Movie Series featuring the "Mighty Morton" theater organ—one of only a few theater organs in the United States still used in its original venue.

This page: The Columbus Zoo and Aquarium houses hundreds of species of mammals, birds, fish, and reptiles from around the globe. Clockwise from top left are Humboldt penguins enjoying a meal, a contemplative gorilla, a drowsy-looking koala, and a very relaxed West Indian manatee.

Facing page: Twin polar bear sisters Aurora and Anana enjoy the sun in the zoo's Polar Frontier. Visitors can watch the bears swimming underwater both from the side and from *underneath* their pool, as the two 500-pound bears fish for trout only a few feet above observers' heads. The area also features Alaskan brown bears Brutus and Buckeye and four arctic foxes.

Left: The fireworks from Columbus's annual Fourth of July celebration, Red, White, and Boom!, erupt above the blue neon arch on the Arena District's outdoor video wall. Anchored by Nationwide Arena, the home of the National Hockey League's Columbus Blue Jackets and a major entertainment venue, the Arena District is a lively destination for dining and nightlife.

Far left: A crowd enjoys Red, White, and Boom! through the elegant Beaux-Arts arch at McPherson Commons in the Arena District. The arch, designed by famed Chicago architect Daniel Burnham, is the only remnant of Union Station, once a major Ohio rail hub. After the station was demolished in 1976, the arch was first rebuilt in 1979 in a small park at Marconi Boulevard and Hickory Street, then moved to its present location in 1998.

Right: Reclaiming the space where a shopping mall once stood, Columbus Commons is a major gathering spot downtown. This nine-acre green space features gardens, a café, a custom-designed carousel, a unique outdoor reading room, and an outdoor performance center.

Below: The 15,000-square-foot fountain at John W. Galbreath Bicentennial Park is a terrific place to cool off on a hot summer day. Nearby are a casual outdoor café and a bandshell for music under the stars. Just to the north, the grand esplanade of the Promenade on the Scioto Mile connects Bicentennial Park to Battelle Riverfront Park, creating a green corridor all along the Scioto River downtown.

This page: Each July the Jazz and Rib Fest brings cool jazz and hot ribs to Columbus. For three days the city's largest free outdoor music festival showcases artists that have included Diane Schuur, Flora Purim, Tito Puente, Jr., (shown at right), Dave Koz, and Big Bad Voodoo Daddy. With three stages, the music never stops!

Facing page: The Columbus Symphony Orchestra (CSO) plays under the baton of music director Jean-Marie Zeitouni. Founded in 1951, today's CSO performs a full schedule of both classical and pop music, including its popular summer Picnic with the Pops outdoor concerts.

Above: Located in Dublin's Scioto Park, *Leatherlips* is a twelve-foot-high portrait of Chief Leatherlips, one of the last of the Wyandot tribe of Native Americans to live in the area. According to local history, Leatherlips was executed nearby by his own tribesmen, either for witchcraft or for his refusal to betray his white friends; accounts differ. Ralph Helmick's sculpture is built of native limestone and features a ramp, accessible from the back of the sculpture, that provides a high point from which to view the Scioto River.

Left: A celebration of a growing suburb's farming past, Malcolm Cochran's *Field of Corn (with Osage Orange Trees)*, fills Dublin's Sam and Eulalia Franz Park with 109 sculptural ears of cast-concrete corn. The Osage orange trees that border the park are also a remnant of farming days: these tough, dense trees once delineated farm fields all over Ohio. The park was the site of the Franz family farm where Sam Frantz worked with The Ohio State University to develop hybridized varieties of corn. This work was commissioned in 1994 by the Dublin Arts Council with support from the City of Dublin.

Following pages: A visitor to the Ohio Veterans' Plaza showcases messages from Ohio veterans. Located on the east side of the Ohio Statehouse, the curved limestone walls are inscribed with excerpts from actual letters written by and for members of the armed forces serving in conflicts.

My Darling,

After chow, we went back to the field and were told that we were to sleep there for the night. I laid my poncho on the very damp ground and put my sleeping bag on top of this and then spread the other half of the poncho over the bag. I wore my green pants, wool shirt, flannel dress shirt, field jacket, wool socks and my silver fox coat. Well, maybe it isn't silver fox but it's fur of some kind, probably field mice. I then climbed into the sleeping bag and zipped it up. The stars were really beautiful. I think I must have slept during the night because I dreamt of you. I probably would have frozen stiff if I hadn't.

All my love forever,
Tom

Darling,

Tonight is Christmas night. There is still no mail from you and I miss your letters very much. Letters have souls; they can speak, they have in them all the fires of our passions, they have all the tenderness, delicacy of speech and sometimes a boldness of expression beyond it.

All of my joys have nothing but the memory of the past. I still preserve the desire to be loved by you. My passion by right belongs to you, and you can in no way become disengaged. A love such as mine cannot be indifferent. I recall your image in my mind. I incessantly seek for you. I shall still love you with all my soul till the last moment of my life. Goodnight, darling.

All my love,
Tommy

Hello Chris,

Prayers were answered when the chemicals we become ineffective as the wind changed and they blew back on Iraqi troops. How astounding!! I am here to give glory to God. I became very disheartened during all of this and wondered would I ever see America again. How are we going to get home? Perhaps on the wings of angels.

Love,
Gail

Dearest Mom and Dad,

I met this S/Sgt. Barry the first day I was in the ward in the "Krankenhaus." Usually the discussions start with combat experiences, but soon our discussion swung from the war to home and the folks back home. Before long I had all my pictures out of my wallet. He was with the 82nd Airborne Div. ever since their first combat jump in North Africa. In all, he jumped all five missions—N.A., Anzio and Salerno, Normandy on D-Day and, finally, Belgium. He was hit in Belgium. He showed me a picture of himself as a civilian and his hair was very dark. Now his hair is snow white and there were also lines of worry on his face.

Oceans of love,
Fritz

Dear Darling,

Yes, I've seen the Iraqi POW's. They're just like normal people. Most were soldiers in their country by threat that if they didn't fight their families would be killed. Most surrendered. So when I find we were returning them, they were killed. It's such a sad story. Then there are the babies that were in the wrong place at the wrong time. I can't wait to come home. Looks like May. Thank the Lord. I'm ready to get back to the good U.S. of A.

Love,
Shirley

...noticing a guy filling his ammo belt with ... once saw a cartoon by Mauldin of two ... fire fight & when trying to get ammo out ... they both had all cigarettes. I saw that ... actually happen once. We were getting ... for ammo.

Love,
Lindy

Dear Dad,

Three days ago, our company was mortared and received grenades and scattered small arms fire. The third platoon leader was killed, the first platoon leader wounded and eighteen others were evacuated. I didn't get a scratch, but I have never been so scared in all my life. Dad, I saw the sunrise that morning and, along with others, sat for hours in disbelief. I must have thanked the Lord a hundred times since for that sunrise.

We headed back. I saw my point man go down. When I got to him he was unconscious, shot through the chest and back. I slapped his face and told him to wake up, this was no time to be sleepin' on the job. He came to, in pain but OK. My RTO did a fine job calling in support. After going through that and seeing how all of these "scared" men become strong, good fighters, you know I can't help but respect their courage. I can't help but love them.

Keep in touch,
Bud

Hi Folks,

We'll be going to the port in a couple of ... pick up our brand new M1A1 Abrams tank ... them earlier this week, super nice, straig... Lima. Go ahead, Baghdad, make my day! ... finally outlived the Vietnam stigma. I p... wither away when the casualties start. T... over here are among the finest, best tra... women who've ever served the nation. T... the challenge with exceptional skill, coura... I am proud to be with them.

As the deadline approaches, please don't ... surprising but I feel pretty calm. I've ... trained my people as best I can—I've ... with the Lord. What ever happens, He ... to be. Been listening to the radio and ... very encouraging. It's hard to believe S... thinks he can best us? Is he nuts? It's ... Three hours til the deadline.

Love to all,
Chip

...sweeping, air strikes were ... 30 PM we found a trail ... passed to "fix bayonets" ... ought it was a joke. Then a ... ped a booby trap grenade and ... wound. The 1st platoon was ... fire from a bunker on top of ... After three hours of fighting, ... platoon took eight dead, ... platoon, seven dead, sixteen ... t, Lima company came up ... ny position.

...nding Independence Day on ... pper is trying to arrange some ... the resupply run today, the ... s, C rations, letter mail ... h fruit, juices, smokes, candy, ... ou can see the Laotian border ... anges and rolling hills. We are ... contact with the enemy because ... force. We are reconnaissing.

D.A.G.

...t Marge,

...does this find my little sis tonight? You were
...ring what the name of my plane was. Its name
...uld say her name) is "Shady Lady" and we have
...picture of a beautiful gal clothed scantily (but
...ently) painted on the side of the nose by me. I'm
...to get a picture taken of the crew beside it one of
days.

Sincerely yours,
George
KIA

Dear Folks,

I stopped on a booby trap April 15. It sent a bullet through my
left calf. It shattered the bone but I kept tellin the Doc not to cut
it off. He did a great job.

Yesterday, a Captain and a SP4 came in and presented me with
the Purple Heart right at the ward. They pinned it to my pillow
where everybody could see it. It brought a tear to my eye.

Take care, pray for me
Sam

Dear Folks,

Well I guess this will be my Christmas letter to all of
you for the year 1970. All who always get together to
celebrate Christ's birthday.

Right now I am sitting on a jungle-covered hilltop - a
setting sun. It is very hard to get in any sort of Christmas
spirit as every day is the same - tromp through the jungle
and hunt poor Charlie. We will be on our firebase for
Christmas, but no matter where we are, everyone's thoughts
will be of home.

In a way, I am thankful of being away from home over the
holidays. It makes you realize just how important family
relationships really are. Vietnam has taught me another thing
also and that is the value of life. It is my firm belief that
God loves Charlie Cong just as much as he loves us. In
war, he is on everyone's side. It is just because the family
of man is so ignorant and selfish and refuses to practice
the love that all religions teach that we have war today.

The other day, we killed a Montagnard. He was called an
enemy as he indeed had a Soviet rifle and was working for
the VC harvesting their rice. No doubt he would have fired
at us had he seen us first. But as I stood looking down at
his bullet-riddled body, covered only by a loin cloth, I felt
only sorrow. He was not my enemy. The VC indoctrinated
him, handed him a rifle and sent him on his way. No, this
'enemy', just like all other war casualties, is a victim.
Man's failure to accept Christ's message, Peace on Earth,
Goodwill Toward Men, the day after Christmas, we all go
back to our selfish ways. Diplomacy has failed to bring
peace. I guess religion is our only hope - that and every
man's willingness to swallow a little pride and replace it
with understanding and love.

Love,
Curt

...mory:

...arachuted into Normandy six hours before D-Day
...s all alone in the dark except for three live cows
...ive bloated dead cows. I sat on a rock and was
...bound by the beautiful fireworks that lit up the
...I felt relaxed and was thinking, "This is a nice
... peaceful war." However, when I saw fiery sparks
...g towards American planes the fireworks lost
...of their beauty.

J.F.

Hi Folks,

It's the day after Christmas here in sunny Saudi. Our
Christmas was not the best I've ever had, but not too
bad. Christmas eve, some of the mechanics came around
singing carols. It was unexpected and did a lot to raise
spirits! My tent mates and I decorated the little tree you
sent, made some of that Wassail stuff (not bad!) and opened
presents. It was a nice, peaceful evening. The pot-bellied stove
and the Christmas candles set a homey atmosphere.

Yesterday, Christmas day, we had Christmas dinner. The
mess hall outdid themselves! We even got the Saudi version
of a White Christmas - a huge sand storm! We told ourselves
it was Saudi snow!

Love you,
Chip

Mom ...

...
...to me and makes the...
...thinking about the...
Regardless of my personal...
...the decisions made by the leaders...
...because I trust in them that...
...actions that will keep our country...
...upon, give my life for that. Trust...
...for the brave men & women here. I...
...my life & soul right now...

...do not open the enclosed letter...
...that you need to open it (you know...
...), please do it in the presence of...
...I will be able to destroy it a few...
...self overcome by... see you the...

Love & prayers,
Rod

Mother and Dad,

...start by saying that my points are now 54 - I got
...one more battle star which the division now
...and 5 more for the Bronze Star. I got it for a
...into enemy lines one night when we were in
the... I remember the exact time because, three
of us... two hours on our stomachs not over 15
feet from a German machine gun nest. It was cold
as hell and I was sweating like it was June.

Right now we are occupying a zone and trying to
get things straightened out between the Russians,
Czechs, Partisans and the peace-loving American
army. We have the Russians near us. They are quite
an outfit, not particularly well dressed soldiers but
they are plenty tough and darn hard to get along with.
They reflect the attitude of Stalin in all actions. And
they trust... about us far as I can throw a horse
but by being diplomatic, we get along and I hope
we'll do the same in the future.

All my love,
Phil

Dear Mom, Dad and All,

It is foggy most of the time and so we see very
little sunshine. I even have to pray for myself once
in a while. You get very jittery not knowing what may
happen. You have only God to turn to for protection
and guidance. Anything can happen and usually does.
You die a thousand times and don't know it. Your
mind wanders and you think about home, your folks,
your girl. Will you ever see them again? Sure you
will! "Nothing will happen to me," you say. "I'll
watch my step." Yeah. You keep on walking, clinging
to your rifle, finger itching on the trigger, waiting,
waiting for something to move in the stinkin' jungle.
It's dark as pitch. Maybe it's just a monkey or an
elephant, or a jungle cat or a snake or one of your
own men who got lost. Or maybe it's the dirty, sneakin',
filthy enemy lying in wait, ready to make a bloody mess
of you. You don't breathe.

Your son,
George

Dear Sis,

She says how...
of bulldozers...
(at home), etc....
while we wash...
home?" she asks...
of laughs out...
Friendly Enemy...
Mom - she'll w...

The water...
bathe in the...
get better late...
fellows think...

Left: The Palm House at the Franklin Park Conservatory and Botanical Gardens is illuminated each day at dusk by artist James Turrell's *Light Raiment II.* The changing colors of this permanent light show lend a magical air to the grand Victorian structure, which opened to the public in 1895. Today, the enlarged Conservatory sits amid ninety-three acres of gardens and hosts events such as the annual Blooms and Butterflies, when hundreds of butterflies are released amid the indoor horticultural displays.

Below: At Topiary Park, the elaborate topiaries of sculptor James T. Mason recreate the Georges Seurat painting *A Sunday Afternoon on the Island of La Grand Jatte,* even including a curly-tailed topiary monkey. Located on the grounds of the old Ohio School for the Deaf and enclosed by an antique iron fence that once surrounded the Ohio Statehouse, the park also offers landscaped walking paths and picnic tables.

Above: Originally named the Ogden Theatre and Ballroom, the Lincoln Theatre opened on Thanksgiving Day in 1928. The grand Egyptian Revival venue was built in a historically African-American area, now called the King-Lincoln District, in response to the segregation of local theaters. Famous in its heyday as a jazz mecca, the fully renovated Lincoln reopened in 2009 as a state-of-the-art urban performing arts center hosting dance, theater, and film programs as well as its signature jazz.

Facing page: The recently redeveloped South Campus Gateway to The Ohio State University features the Gateway Film Center, shopping, and restaurants for every taste. New investment in the area has brought renewed vitality to OSU's south campus area.

Left: The Easton Town Center shopping complex pioneered the new wave of outdoor shopping malls. Designed on the model of a small town, Easton offers full-scale department stores, small boutiques, unique restaurants, and family-friendly green spaces. These children toss beach balls in the cooling water of a fountain.

Below: Owned by the Columbus Zoo and Aquarium, Zoombezi Bay is nearly twenty-three acres of summer fun. Visitors can cool off on seventeen water rides, float the lazy river, or ride the waves in a 544,500-gallon wave pool. And this waterpark isn't just for kids; grownups have their own island at Zoombezi Bay—Croctail Island, with lounging decks, food, and beverages just for adults.

Right: A swirl of colorful skirts accompanies El Corazón de México Ballet Folklórico's traditional dance at the Festival Latino. For more than fifteen years, Columbus has celebrated Latino culture each summer with food, art, music, and fun in the sun. In recent years, a new emphasis on local visual artists has revealed the rich veins of Latino culture found in Ohio and the Columbus area.

Below: For more than twenty-five years, the Short North Arts District's Doo Dah Parade has celebrated free speech and inspired silliness. A highly democratic event, past parades have included these "potheads," the Marching Fidels, the Push Mower Brigade, a small pig with an incredibly overfull bladder, and a police patrol car driven backward. It may be hilarious, satirical, or just plain wacky, but the Doo Dah Parade is never dull.

Left: Henry Moore's bronze figure study *Three Piece Reclining Figure: Draped* graces the lawn of the Columbus Museum of Art (CMA). A frequent host to traveling exhibitions, the museum also boasts an outstanding permanent collection of nineteenth- and twentieth-century American and European art. CMA is nationally recognized for its strong regional collections, including the woodcarvings of local folk artist Elijah Pierce and the world's largest collection of paintings and lithographs by Columbus native George Bellows.

Below, left: A whimsical bronze sculpture titled *The Unicorn in the Garden,* by Jack Greaves, gazes across Jefferson Avenue at the Thurber House and Museum, former home of writer and cartoonist James Thurber. Thurber's somewhat eccentric family lived here while he attended The Ohio State University, and several of his short stories are set in the house, including "The Night the Ghost Got In" and "The Night the Bed Fell." Today the Thurber House offers a residency program for children's writers, author readings, and writing classes.

Below, right: The soaring bronze and stainless steel form of Stephen Canneto's *Intersect* embodies the intersections of culture, commerce, community, nature, and technology. Commissioned in celebration of the Huntington Bank's 126th year in business, the sculpture fittingly stands where High Street, once part of a Native American trail, intersects Broad Street, a part of the old National Road that carried white settlers west.

Following pages: Since the first Ohio State Fair was forced to cancel in 1849 due to a cholera epidemic, the event has grown to epic proportions. Now held at the Ohio Expo Center north of downtown Columbus, the Fair is a twelve-day extravaganza of agricultural exhibitions, music, rides, and the ubiquitous fair food. Here, the cool backdrop of the city's skyline accentuates the color and motion of the midway, as seen from the Ohio Historical Society building.

Above, left and right: Colorful regional costumes are a popular part of the yearly Asian Festival. Since its debut in 1995, the festival has grown steadily; more than 100,000 visitors each year now enjoy its traditional and contemporary Asian performing arts, cultural exhibitions, games, martial arts, and food.

Left: The elaborate dress and brilliant smiles of traditional Irish dancers light up the Dublin Irish Festival. Held each year in early August, the event features local and internationally known Celtic musicians on multiple stages, traditional bagpipe bands, darts, storytelling, shopping, and, of course, Irish beer. *Slainte!*

Right: Each June more than 200 artists from all over the United States gather in Columbus to display and sell their wares at the Columbus Arts Festival. The all-juried event is well known for the quality and variety of its offerings, as well as its convivial atmosphere and great food. Admission is free, and visitors can check out offerings from drawings to didgeridoos—or just spend an afternoon people-watching.

Below, left: The North Market features fresh produce, meats, poultry, and fish as well as cheeses, handcrafted chocolates, and prepared foods. The Market is a popular place to grab a quick lunch, and on summer Saturdays the outdoor farmer's market draws vendors and buyers from throughout the area in a celebration of fresh, local food.

Below, right: The Claddagh Irish Pub is only one of many attractions in the Brewery District. When German immigrants flooded into Columbus in the mid-nineteenth century, they founded a number of breweries along High and Front streets south of downtown. Though pasteurization and refrigerated rail cars eventually spelled the end for the local breweries, many of the old buildings have been renovated as restaurants and entertainment spots—including several microbreweries that carry on the area's tradition.

Right: A grand celebration of the Fourth of July, the fireworks of Red, White, and Boom! light up the Columbus sky above the LeVeque Tower, dressed in its holiday lights of red, white, and blue.

Below, left: COSI, the Center of Science and Industry, has been a Columbus institution since 1964. Poseidon, the king of the sea, rules over the Oceans exhibit, where visitors learn about both the physical nature of water and ocean exploration technology.

Below, right: Poseidon appears to be pointing to some rather interesting characters. The Mad Hatter and his friends are enjoying Halloween HighBall in the Short North Arts District. The event combines a competition for professional clothing designers with costumed craziness for adults and children, Short North style.

Right, top: Conceived as a laboratory for performing and visual art, Ohio State's Wexner Center for the Arts opened in 1989. Today the Wex is known for its cutting-edge visual exhibitions, edgy performance art, and video and film presentations. The building's unique architecture repeats elements of the university armory that once occupied the site; the large tower structure shown echoes the older building's main tower.

Right, bottom: The Jerome Schottenstein Center is the home of The Ohio State University men's and women's basketball and men's hockey programs, as well as a leading central-Ohio concert and events venue. An interesting fact: the facility's "elephant door" not only lets elephants enter the building without ducking their heads, but also allows semi trucks and tour buses access to the arena floor.

Far right: University Hall at The Ohio State University is actually the second building by that name on the same site. The original was built in 1873 and served as classrooms, student dormitory, and faculty housing for the fledgling Ohio Agricultural and Mechanical College. That building was demolished in 1972 and replaced by the current University Hall—the exterior of which is a near duplicate of the original.

This panoramic view of the Columbus skyline, as seen from the roof of the Condominiums at North Bank Park, encompasses most of the city's downtown. Part of Nationwide Arena, including its light tower, is visible at the far left, and the Ohio Judicial Center can be seen at the far right; other major buildings shown include (from left) the Hyatt Regency Hotel, two buildings in the Nationwide Plaza complex, the William Green Building, the AEP Building, the James A. Rhodes State Office Tower, the Hyatt on Capitol Square, the LeVeque Tower, the Huntington Center, and the Vern Riffe State Office Tower. The green space and several of the buildings in the left foreground occupy part of the former Ohio Penitentiary site.

Left: The magnificent lobby of the Palace Theatre was inspired by Louis XIV's palace in Versailles. Located at the base of the LeVeque Tower, the Palace was originally intended for vaudeville, and its outstanding acoustics still serve it well as a popular concert and theater venue.

Below, left: The sweeping Grand Staircase at the east entrance to the Senate Building was modeled after the Paris Opera House. The Senate Building was built on the east side of the Ohio Statehouse and today is connected to it by an enclosed atrium. The entire complex was renovated in 1996, removing a labyrinth of small offices and returning both buildings to their original beauty.

Below, right: The Ohio Statehouse rotunda rises 120 feet from its intricate marble floor (made up of more than 5,000 hand-cut pieces of marble) to a replica of the original 1849 stained-glass Ohio State Seal at the top of the dome. Abraham Lincoln spoke at the Statehouse in 1859 and 1861. After his assassination in 1865, more than 50,000 mourners filed past his coffin in just six-and-a-half hours as he lay in state here in the rotunda—especially impressive considering the entire population of central Ohio at the time was about 31,000.

Right: A Victorian gazebo seems to rise from a sea of lotus blossoms in this view of Goodale Park. Located in the heart of the Victorian Village neighborhood, the park encompasses forty acres of land donated by Dr. Lincoln Goodale, Columbus pioneer and the city's first physician. Under the terms of Dr. Goodale's bequest, the land must remain a "public park or pleasure resort" or revert to his heirs.

Below: Just west of its confluence with the Scioto River, Hayden Run has carved out a jewel-like gorge where Hayden Falls tumbles into a clear pool and woodland plants thrive. Though surrounded on three sides by homes and heavily-traveled suburban streets, the gorge remains surprisingly tranquil and hushed, a suburban "secret garden." A stairway and boardwalk provide access while protecting the gorge's delicate ecosystem, which includes several rare and endangered plants.

Left: Since 1980 the Columbus Marathon has drawn both amateur and elite athletes to its run through the streets of Columbus. In recent years the marathon has drawn nearly 15,000 participants.

Below: For nearly twenty years, the Tour de Grandview Cycling Classic has drawn an international field of professional bicyclists to suburban Grandview Heights. The annual event includes children's activities and a street party as well as USA Cycling-sanctioned racing action on hilly, tree-lined suburban streets.

Far left: The annual New Albany Classic Invitational Grand Prix and Family Day is an internationally sanctioned horse-jumping event in which thirty riders compete for $100,000 in prizes. Held at the New Albany estate of Limited Brands founder and CEO Leslie Wexner, the event also features a variety of family entertainment. Ticket proceeds benefit the Columbus Coalition Against Family Violence.

Right: Huntington Park, the home field of the Class AAA International League Columbus Clippers, opened in 2009 in the Arena District. Huntington Park incorporates "green" building practices, from its site on a former urban brownfield to design features that eliminate the need for air conditioning in all but the locker rooms, press box, and dugout.

Below: Quality baseball, affordable ticket prices, picnic terraces, and a family lawn make Huntington Park a favorite spot for family outings, with many fans coming well before the game just to enjoy the park. Here, the crowd keeps its collective eye on the ball.

Left: The Jack Nicklaus Museum honors one of central Ohio's most celebrated sons. Nicklaus grew up in Upper Arlington and played collegiate golf at The Ohio State University. The winner of eighteen professional golf majors and the designer of the Muirfield Village Golf Club in Dublin, Nicklaus remains a strong presence in the Columbus area.

Below: About 200,000 people visit the Columbus Museum of Art each year to enjoy both traveling exhibitions and the museum's outstanding permanent collection. The collection embraces diverse periods, media, and styles and includes such gems as the Photo League collection, which features the work of photog-raphers Berenice Abbott, W. Eugene Smith, and mysterious New York photojournalist Weegee.

Facing page: Polaris Fashion Place, located just north of downtown Columbus, draws shoppers from all over Ohio. Several of the mall's 150 specialty stores and six anchors are found nowhere else in Columbus. Shoppers enjoy the mall's bright concourses, large indoor playground area, and variety of food choices, including a food court and four full-service restaurants.

Left: Each Labor Day weekend, the Greek Festival at Annunciation Greek Orthodox Cathedral celebrates the best of Greek culture. In addition to watching the Greek Festival Dancers perform in full traditional dress, visitors can shop at a Greek agora, tour the cathedral, view art and craft exhibits, and, of course, eat delicious Greek food. Dolmades and spanakopita, souvlaki and baklava—the Greek Festival is a food lover's heaven.

Below: The Goodale Park Community Festival, or ComFest, describes itself as "three days of alternative politics, art and crafts, music, reunions with old friends, and introductions to new ones." Founded in 1972, ComFest retains its early counterculture underpinnings, political activism, and concern with community needs while presenting more than 200 local musicians and performers each year. Jamming on guitar are Dave Workman, John Boerstler and Johnny Ace.

Left: One of the largest public rose gardens in the country, the Park of Roses showcases nearly 12,000 roses of more than 400 varieties. Arranged to show the history of the rose, the gardens include everything from "old roses" such as damasks and rugosas to the newest low-care "earth kind" types. Wide, level walks invite visitors to enjoy the heady fragrance and delicious colors of thousands of roses in full bloom.

Below, left and right: Costumed visitors to Topiary Park seem to bring the nineteenth-century tableau to life as they enjoy the gardens surrounding topiary figures from Georges Seurat's *A Sunday Afternoon on the Island of La Grand Jatte.* At right is a unique topiary boat in a real pond.

Right: Humorist James Thurber was well known for his whimsical cartoons of dogs. Here, a playful hound springs to sculpted life on the front lawn of the Thurber House, appearing to invite the Capitol Square doughboy (in image at far right) to join in a playful romp.

Far right: Arthur Ivone's *The Doughboy* guards the west entrance to the Ohio Statehouse, gazing out over a Columbus that, from his viewpoint, has changed only slightly since the statue was placed here in 1930. From left, the Huntington Bank Building, the LeVeque Tower, and 8 on the Square, peeking from above the trees at the right, preceded the doughboy statue. Only the venerable Deshler Hotel on the northwest corner of Broad and High streets is gone, replaced in 1987 by the glittering glass of One Columbus Center.

These pages: The Scioto Mile creates a striking recreational area along the downtown riverfront, connecting Battelle Riverfront Park to the north with the John W. Galbreath Bicentennial Park. Visitors can take a sedate stroll on the Promenade along the Scioto River, enjoy lunch at the outdoor café, catch an outdoor performance at the bandshell— or spend a steamy midsummer afternoon frolicking in the Bicentennial Park fountains with a colorful amphibian friend.

Left: Though considerably less well known than the western wonder that shares its name, Ohio's Hoover Dam creates one of the best fishing lakes in Ohio. Located in the Westerville area, Hoover Reservoir and its neighbor to the northwest, Alum Creek Reservoir, provide a variety of year-round recreation opportunities. Here, a tranquil sunrise heralds another beautiful day of fishing and boating at Hoover Reservoir.

Below: One of Ohio's major rivers, the Scioto flows from its headwaters in western Ohio through Columbus on its way to the Ohio River at Portsmouth. Once an important means of travel, today the Scioto is used primarily as a source of drinking water and for recreational purposes. The name "Scioto" comes from the Shawnee word for deer; this group of late-afternoon rowers may well spot a few of the river's namesakes on these banks near the confluence of the Scioto and Olentangy rivers.

Right: A pair of familiar American faces gets a new twist in the Short North Arts District. In Mike Altman and Steve Galgas's 2002 take on Grant Wood's *American Gothic*, the straitlaced farm wife is literally turned on her head.

Below: The most iconic face of the Short North gazes benignly from the side of the Mona Lisa Condominiums. Originally painted by Brian Clemons in 1990, the mural irreverently turns Leonardo DaVinci's famous image of *La Gioconda* on its side in quirky Short North style.

Far right: Also in the Short North is this window display capturing the glittering spirit of masquerade, with a selection of masks to disguise the faces of everyday life.

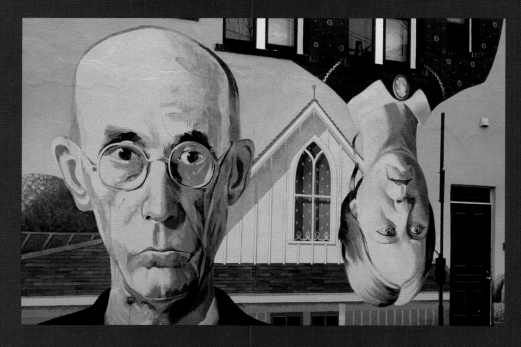

70

Left: Dale Chihuly's glass sculpture *Torchiere* rises from a bed of greenery at Franklin Park Conservatory and Botanical Gardens. After a 2003 Chihuly exhibition here, the Friends of the Conservatory purchased a large number of the works displayed to create the largest permanent collection owned by a conservatory or botanical garden. Chihuly's sinuous, organic glass forms can be seen throughout the Conservatory.

Far left: At Inniswood Metro Gardens, wisteria blooms spill from a curving arbor, framing the gazebo beyond. The heart of Inniswood is the thirty-seven-acre former estate of Grace and Mary Innis, sisters who enjoyed gardening and watching the wildlife on their Westerville property. Today Inniswood totals 121 acres of woodlands, streams, and formal gardens.

Above: This graceful kneeling unicorn is a part of the sculpture garden surrounding the James W. Barney Children's Fountain. The unicorn and its neighbors—a lion, a dog, an owl, and a griffin—figure in the story of a Native American child, Pickaweekee, which is related on plaques in the park. Glass-block waterfalls complete this charming area, a part of the downtown Battelle Riverfront Park.

Right: Victorian Village, a thriving urban neighborhood just north of downtown Columbus, features grand old homes from the Victorian era as well as smaller American vernacular frame homes from the first two decades of the twentieth century. Pedestrian-friendly and boasting a highly diverse population, the rejuvenated Village is one of the most desirable areas of Columbus.

Left: North Bank Park offers a fabulous view of the city skyline, as well as access to the Scioto Greenway trail, which runs along the downtown riverfront to the south and connects with the Olentangy Greenway to the north. Fountains and broad green lawns make North Bank an inviting place to enjoy lunch. Visitors can learn about Columbus history, too—plaques throughout the park relate historical stories, and the stone veneer on the park's walls is recycled from the old Ohio Penitentiary, which once faced the park area.

Below: Two cyclists enjoy a tranquil fall day in Alexander AEP Park. A section of the Scioto Greenway, this bike trail follows the Scioto River through downtown Columbus and will soon connect to an eleven-mile greenway to Griggs Reservoir, northwest of downtown.

Right: The home of the National Hockey League's Columbus Blue Jackets, Nationwide Arena opened its doors to the public in September 2000. The arena is a first-class sports and entertainment venue with luxury features such as open concourses that allow a view into the bowl, elegant terrazzo floors, a glass-enclosed atrium, and a 135-foot light tower. The surrounding Arena District is one of the city's liveliest dining and entertainment destinations.

Below: The American and Ohio flags fly in front of the Vern Riffe State Office Tower and the Huntington Center. The Ohio flag's shape is unique among state flags; properly called a burgee, the flag tapers to two points like a swallow's tail.

Randall Lee Schieber

Based in Columbus, Ohio, Randall Lee Schieber has been a professional photographer for more than twenty years. Schieber was born in Findlay, Ohio, and spent his early childhood in Mexico City. He studied photography and art, first in Tucson, Arizona, and later at The Ohio State University. He went on to earn a BA degree from Kent State University, Kent, Ohio.

Schieber's work appears in five other books on Ohio and Columbus: *Ohio Simply Beautiful, Ohio Impressions, Ohio Then and Now, Columbus, Ohio: A Photographic Portrait* and *Beauty in the Grove: Spring Grove Cemetery and Arboretum.* His work has appeared in a variety of publications, including *Ohio Magazine, Midwest Living,* and the *New York Times.* Many of Schieber's images are on display at Columbus's Sears Distribution Center and McDonald's restaurants, as well as at several Cleveland medical facilities. He has published numerous calendars on Columbus and is featured exclusively each year in the Ohio Scenic Calendar. To view more of Schieber's work, please visit his website at www.randallschieber.com.